This delightful book is the latest in the series of Ladybird books which have been specially planned to help grown-ups with the world about them.

As in the other books in this series, the large clear script, the careful choice of words, the frequent repetition and the thoughtful matching of text with pictures all enable grown-ups to think they have taught themselves to cope. The subject of the book will greatly appeal to grown-ups.

Series 999

THE LADYBIRD
BOOKS FOR GROWN–UPS SERIES

THE QUIET
NIGHT IN

by

J.A. HAZELEY, N.S.F.W. and J.P. MORRIS, O.M.G.

(Authors of 'Setting Your Shadow Free')

Publishers: Ladybird Books Ltd., Loughborough
Printed in England. If wet, Italy.

People are social animals and like to be with other people.

But sometimes we all need a little quiet time, perhaps after a hard day at work or a particularly refreshing lunch.

Or perhaps after just putting the children to bed for the third time.

Getting ready for a night out can take Melissa up to an hour.

Getting ready for a quiet night in takes under twenty seconds, or a minute if it is a posh night in, with trousers.

So far this evening, Margarine has put toothpaste on a spot and eaten a whole bag of Bombay Mix.

Now she is bingeing on back—to—back episodes of Honey I Bought A Boat, with her eyes closed.

"Carpe diem," thinks Margarine.

As we grow older, "fish–fingers and an early night" stops being a punishment and becomes a treat.

This New Year's Eve, Gleb is staying in with a wine box and a Jools Holland Hootenanny in which he does not recognise anyone except Jools Holland.

He falls asleep on the sofa at ten to midnight and misses the bongs.

He has still had a better New Year than anyone fighting to get a taxi home from a ticket–only town–centre pub.

Middle age has its privileges.

Marianne has been staying in watching old episodes of Sex And The City for two weeks now.

The women in the show remind Marianne of her and her friends.

Except that the women in Sex And The City never stay in for two weeks watching old episodes of Sex And The City.

There is a pop disco at the community centre tonight, but the word "community" brings Davey out in a cold sweat.

Some people suffer from F.O.M.O., the fear of missing out.

Davey is delighted that he has F.O.J.I., the fear of joining in.

Just like humans, hedgehogs sometimes like to curl into a ball and sleep for a very long time.

Unlike humans they do not finish the leftover ouzo at the back of the drinks cabinet first.

Riya and Gus are about to put the children to bed. Thursday night is date night.

They will spend forty minutes going through the Netflix menu, not deciding on anything.

Then they will fall asleep.

It is good to have some time to yourself.

Vaughn is staying in and doing some reading. He has a pile of books he has been meaning to read since Christmas.

He reads and he reads and he reads. He reads for hours.

Then he looks up from his phone. It is nearly bedtime.

So he opens one of the books.

Iain does like a quiet night in.

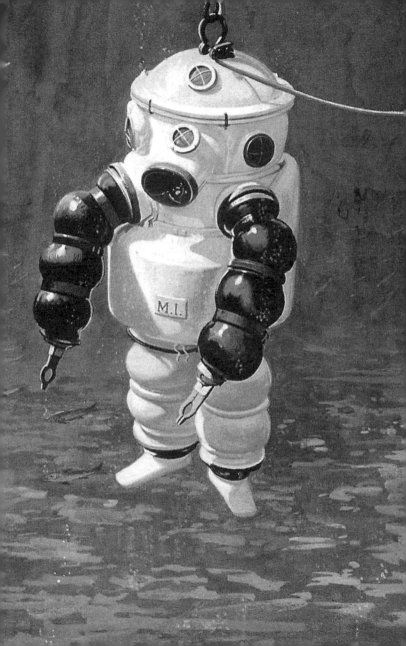

Orga and Kong refuse all social invitations that involve leaving their house. Their friends come to them for dinner instead.

They save money on eating and drinking out. They save money on trains and taxis and petrol. They save money on baby–sitters.

"Bring a bottle", they tell their friends. "And some nibbles."

They have not served an actual dinner in years.

Today's homes boast every modern convenience. Is it any wonder so many people like a quiet night in?

There is television. There is coffee and magazines. There are books and furnitures.

This home even has a robot space witch filled with hot strawberries.

Who needs to go out?

Lynda booked two tables at the Egg and Crown pub for her birthday party.

She has spent three weeks worrying that nobody will come whilst also worrying that everybody will come, and there will not be enough space.

The stress has given her a cold sore so she stays at home in a horrible mood until her flatmates return with cake.

Darius and Ronco have decided to spend the evening in their hammocks watching YouTube.

Their previous plan was to spend the evening down the skate park watching YouTube.

All the latest cinema films on Oswald's home streaming service seem to be aimed at teenagers with no attention span.

"This is why I never pay to go to the cinema," laughs Oswald.

Which is why none of the cinema films are made for people like Oswald.

In her twenties, Andrea would have spent most Saturday nights dancing until daybreak to Belgian nose—bleed techno in a shed.

Tonight, Andrea is staying in to try out her new hoover. The motor is so quiet she can hear Radio 3.

On this many pills, it all sounds incredible.

In 1961, US astronaut Brek Readison broke the record for the longest continuous quiet night in, spending 52 hours in geostationary orbit on the dark side of the moon with a pile of Sunday supplements.

On splash-down, he refused to emerge from the capsule until he had finished his bath.

Kitteridge is doing Dry January and staying in a lot more.

"Dry" is the perfect word for how conversations down the pub sound now he is not drinking.

Clytemnestra has been trying on different outfits and putting things in her hair all evening.

If she sets off now, by the time she gets to the Colosseum, all the Christians will have been eaten.

"I'll just stay in and watch this mosaic I'm into," she decides, and opens an amphora of Lambrini.

Mordecai and four friends are seeing how close to the wire they can all cancel a social drink they have had planned for over a month.

Working late. Childcare. Family commitments. They have all thought of clever reasons.

The last to call is the loser. Nobody wants to look like the sort of person who has nothing else in their life except fun.

Jesmond is burying a batch of his home—brewed hollyhock and cardamom champagne in the garden where it can calm down a bit.

Drinking home—made beer and wine in your own home is a good way of saving money and putting you off beer and wine.

Domingo is having yet another quiet night in.

His friends are going out to drink mead and consider the lilies, but Domingo wants to stay in and wash the sides of his hair.

Julia does not want to go out to eat. She does not want to cook. She does not even want to order anything off this take–away menu because it would mean getting up to answer the door in her backup pyjamas and speaking.

"I've got some left–overs in a bag from last night," she thinks.

If there are no witnesses, two nights of crisps for dinner is probably fine.

THE AUTHORS would like to record their gratitude and offer their apologies to the many Ladybird artists whose luminous work formed the glorious wallpaper of countless childhoods. Revisiting it for this book as grown-ups has been a privilege.

MICHAEL JOSEPH

UK | USA | Canada | Ireland | Australia
India | New Zealand | South Africa

Michael Joseph is part of the Penguin Random House group of companies whose addresses can be found at global.penguinrandomhouse.com

First published 2017
001

Copyright © Jason Hazeley and Joel Morris, 2017
All images copyright © Ladybird Books Ltd, 2017

The moral right of the authors has been asserted

Printed in Italy by L.E.G.O. S.p.A

A CIP catalogue record for this book is available from the British Library

ISBN: 978–0–718–18868–9

www.greenpenguin.co.uk

MIX
Paper from
responsible sources
FSC® C018179
www.fsc.org

Penguin Random House is committed to a sustainable future for our business, our readers and our planet. This book is made from Forest Stewardship Council® certified paper.